Cute Valentines Doodles

Valentines day coloring books for adults

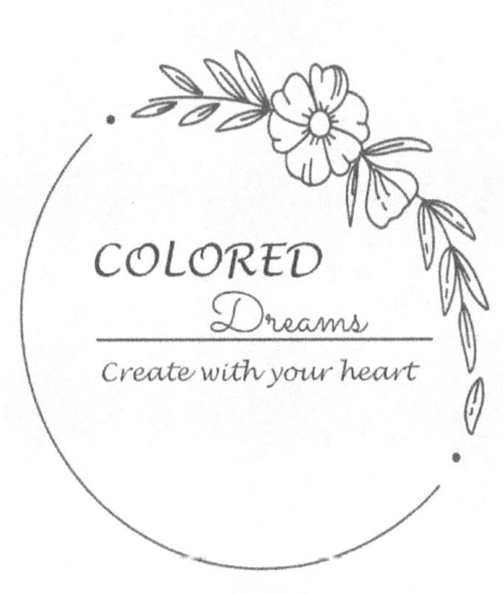

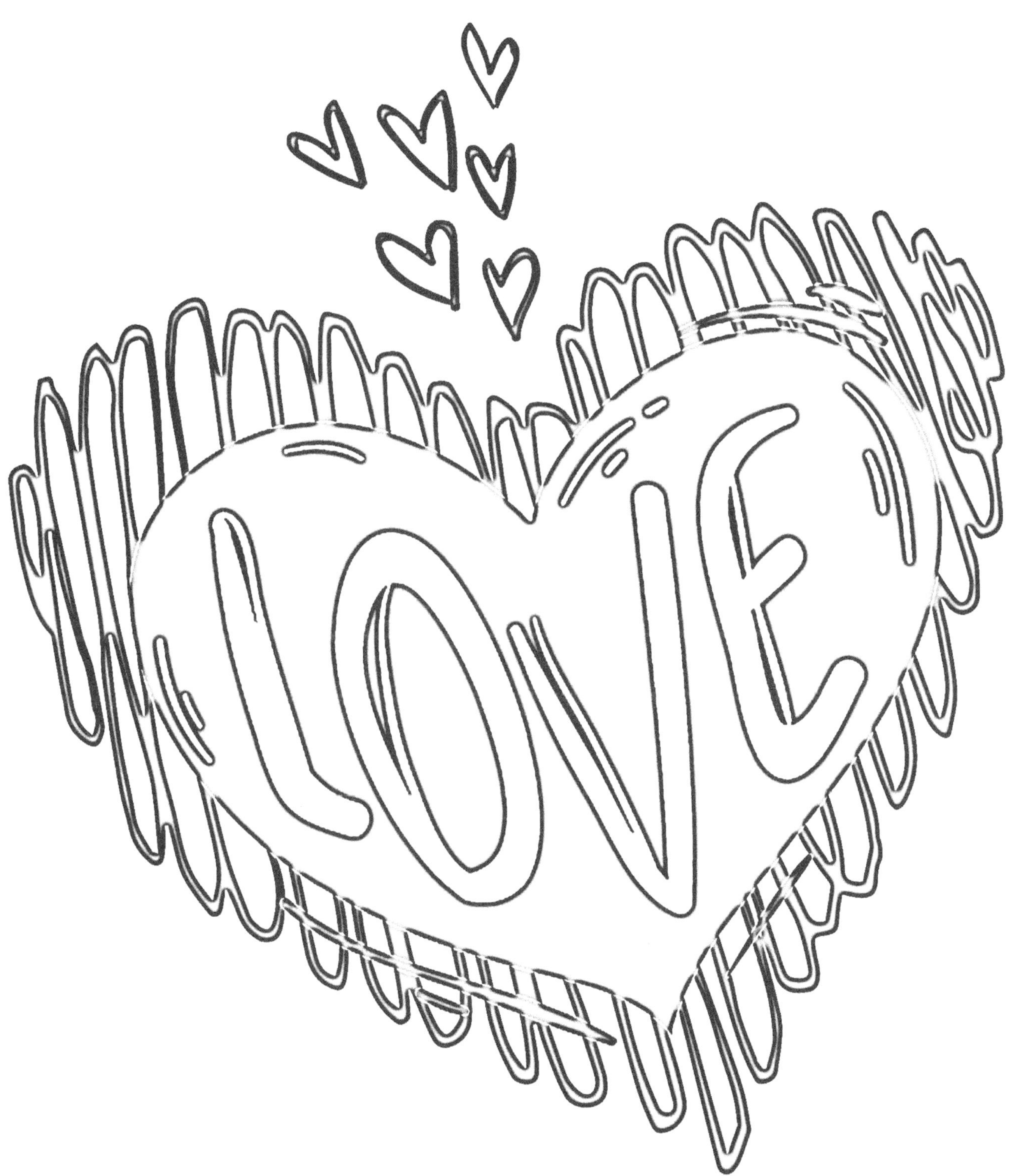

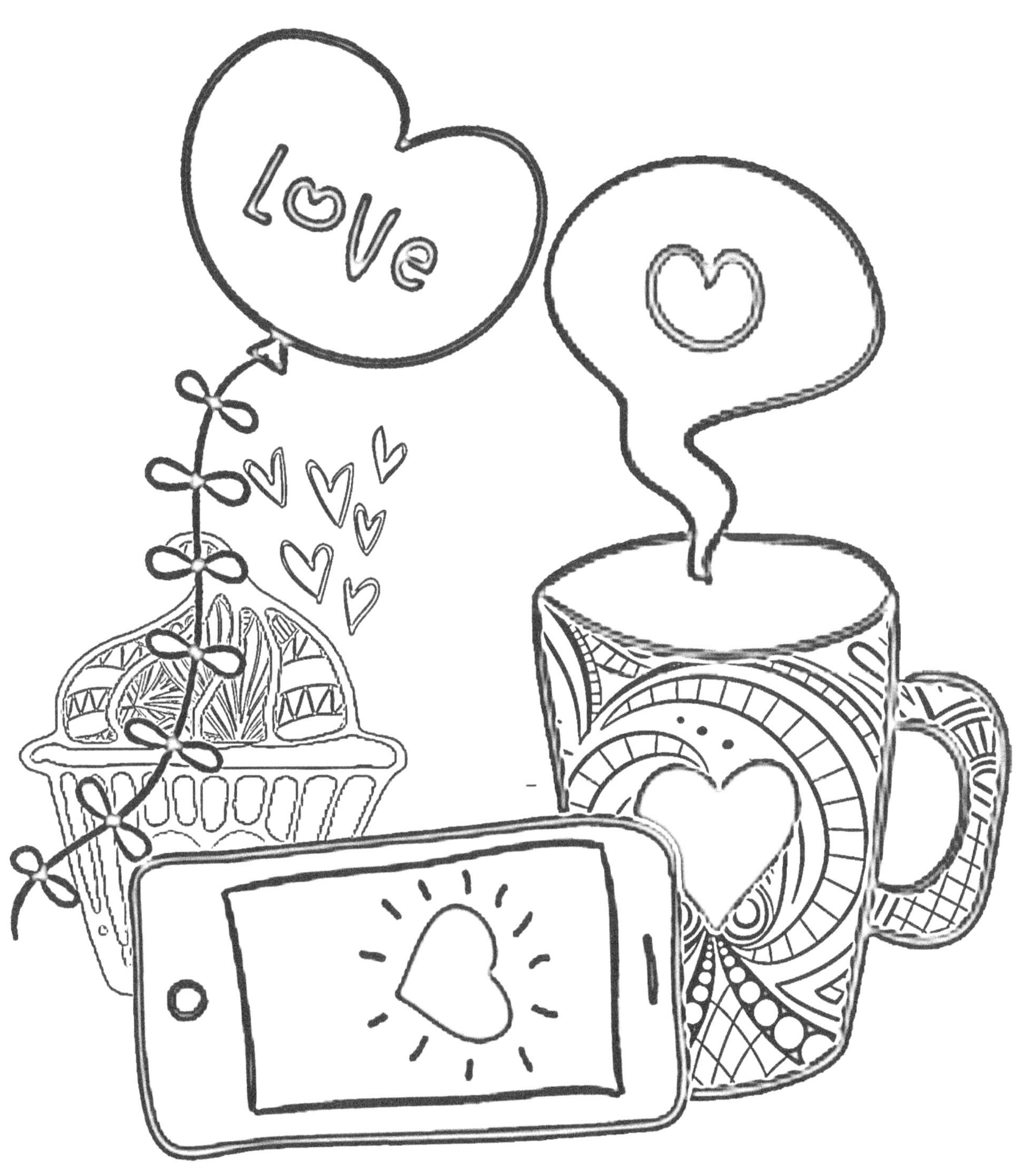
Love

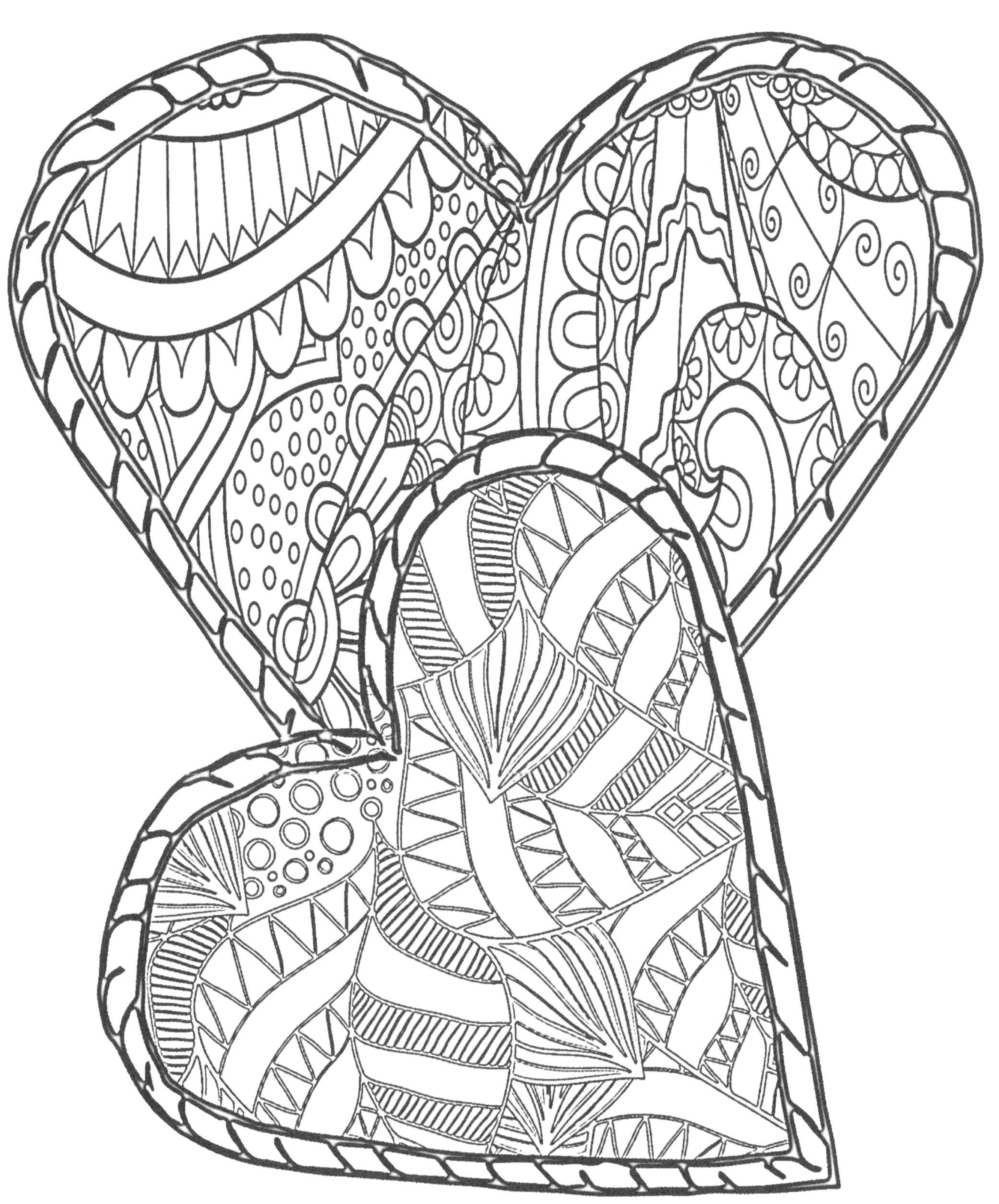

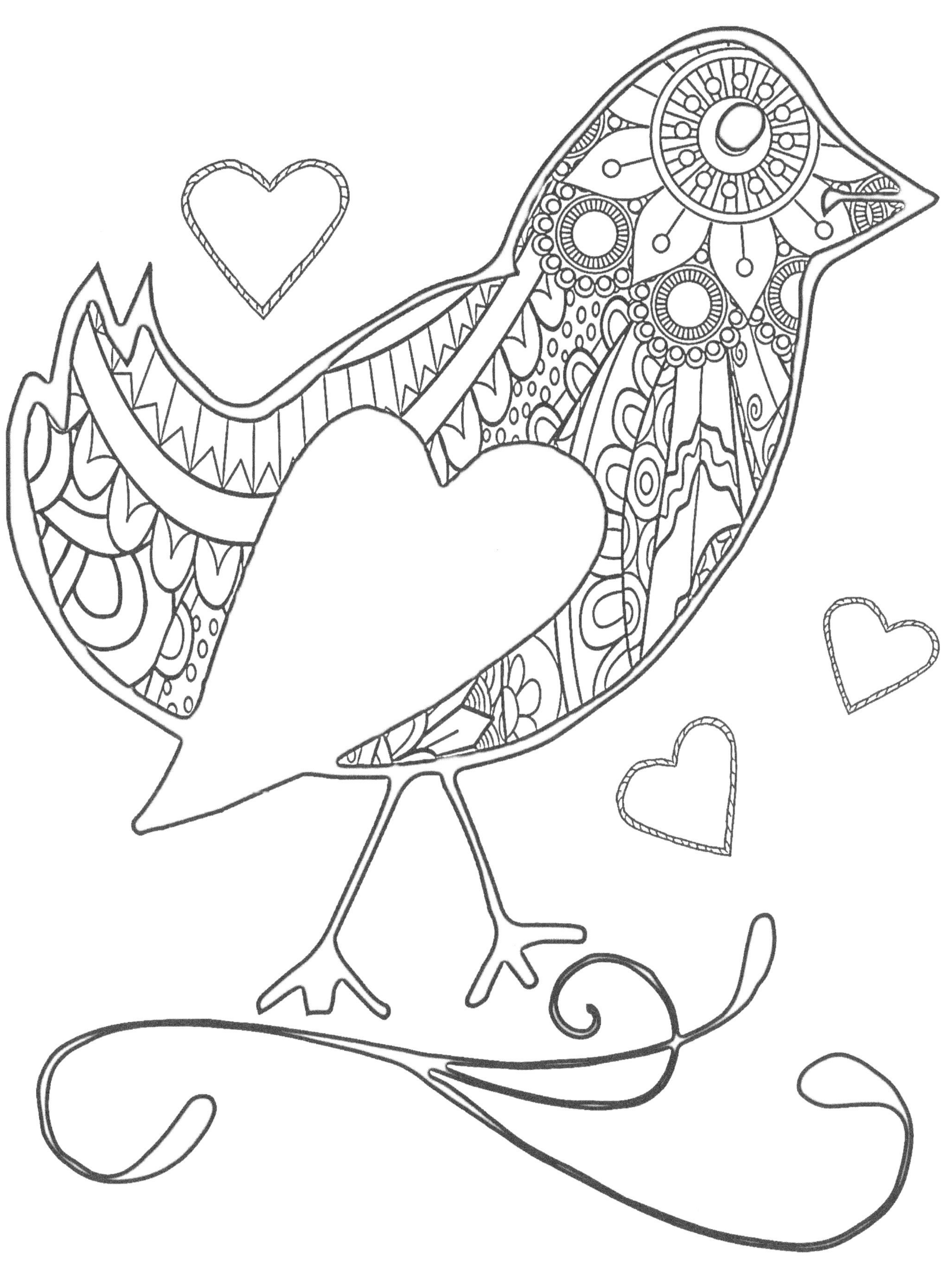

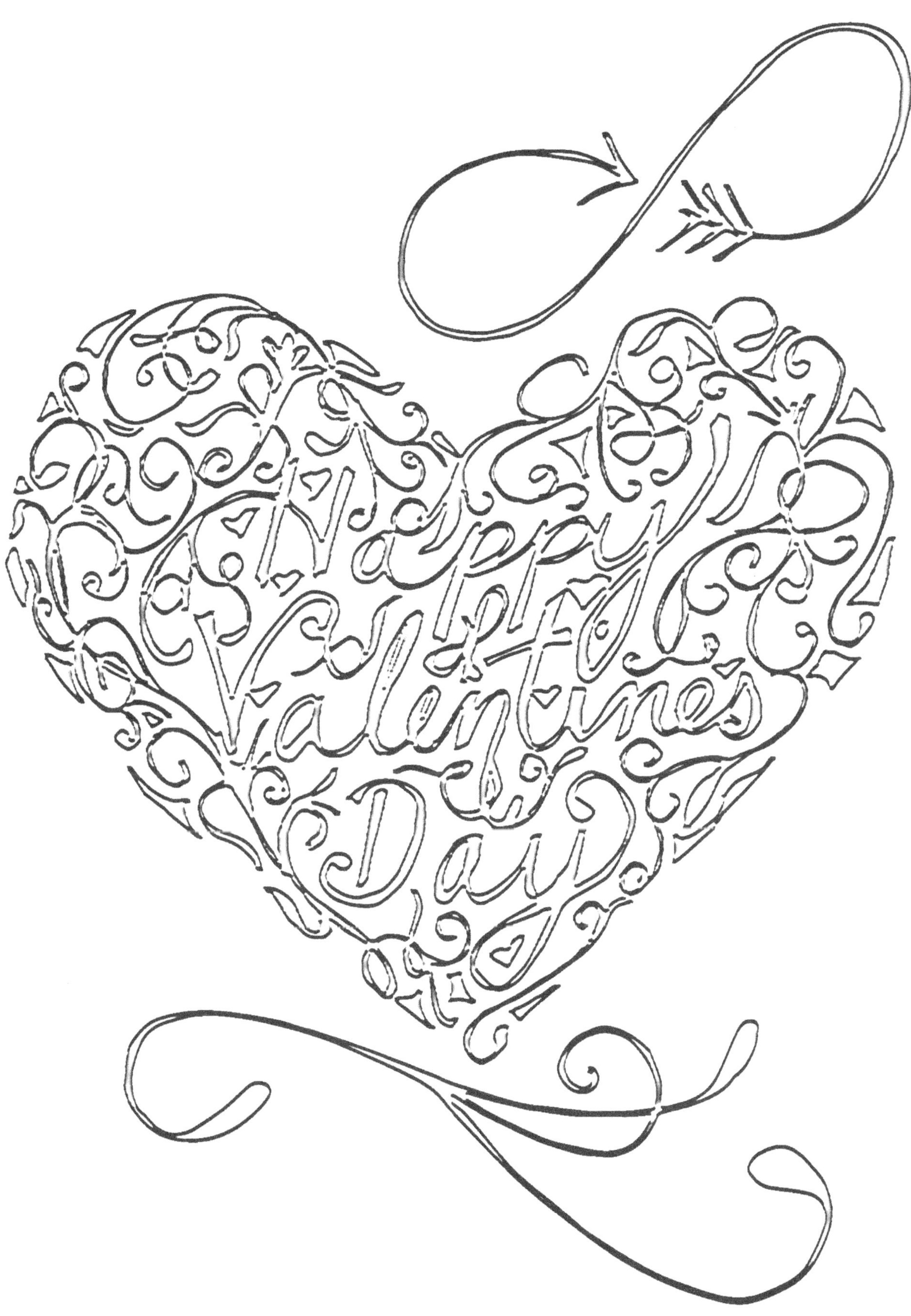
Happy Valentine's Day

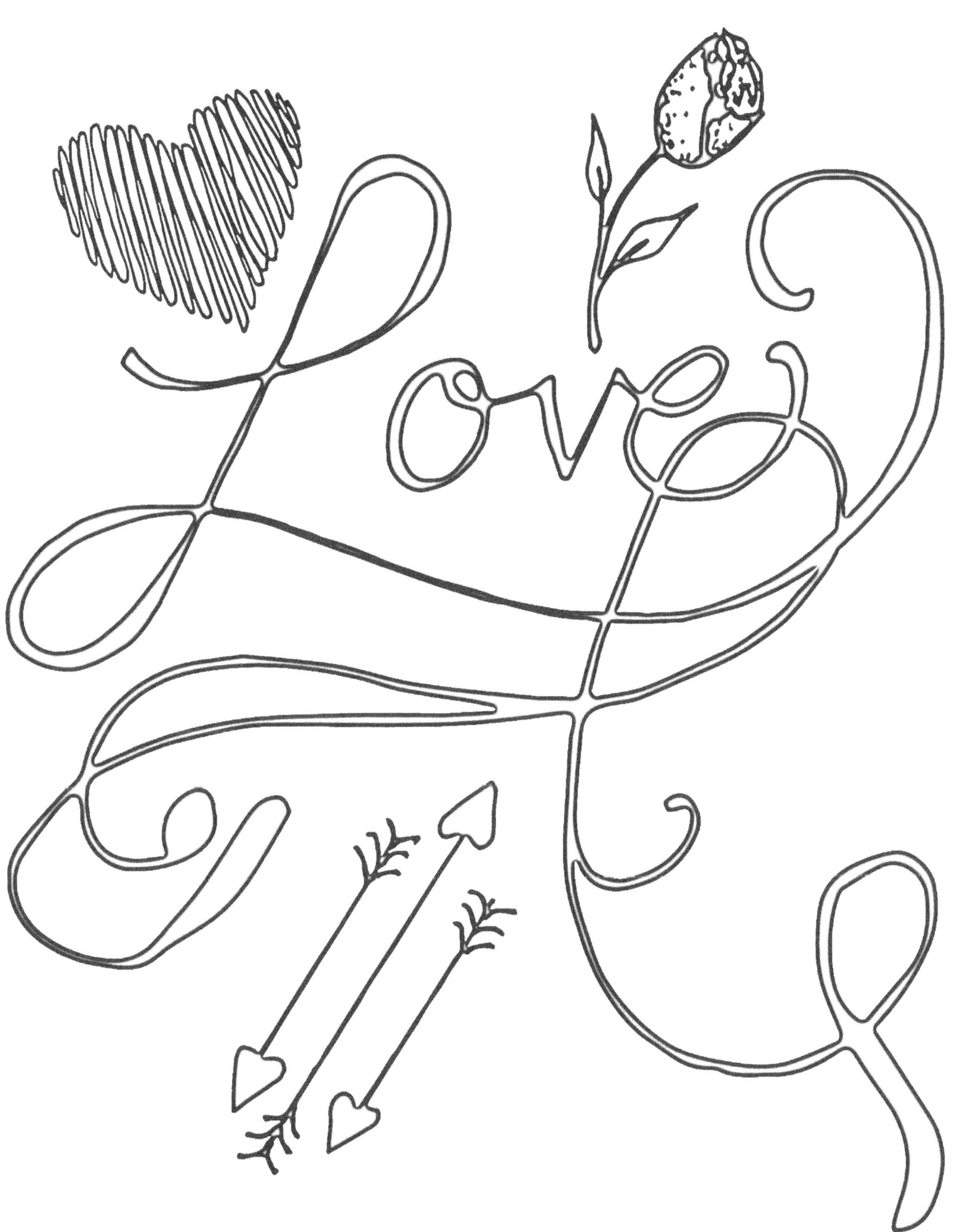

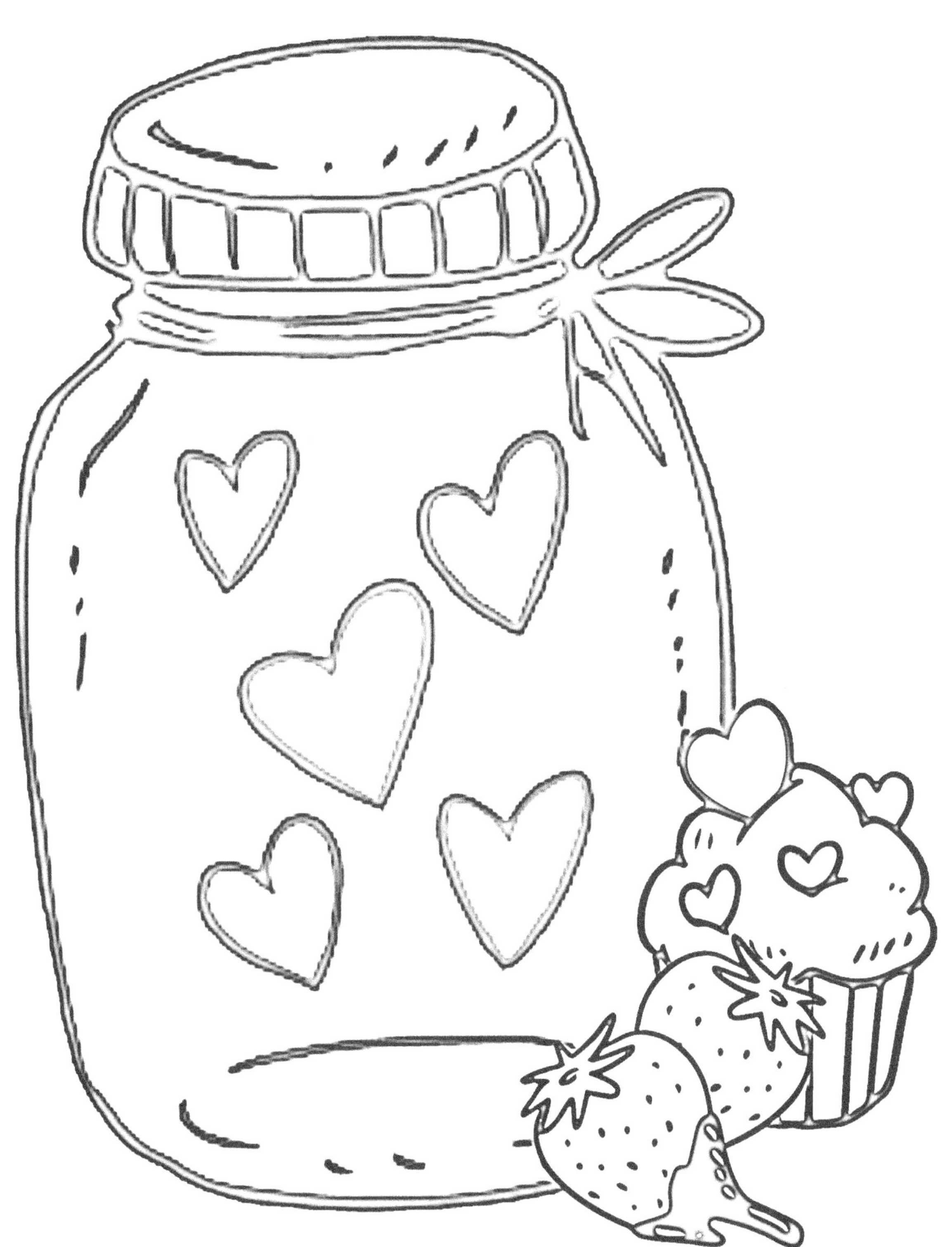

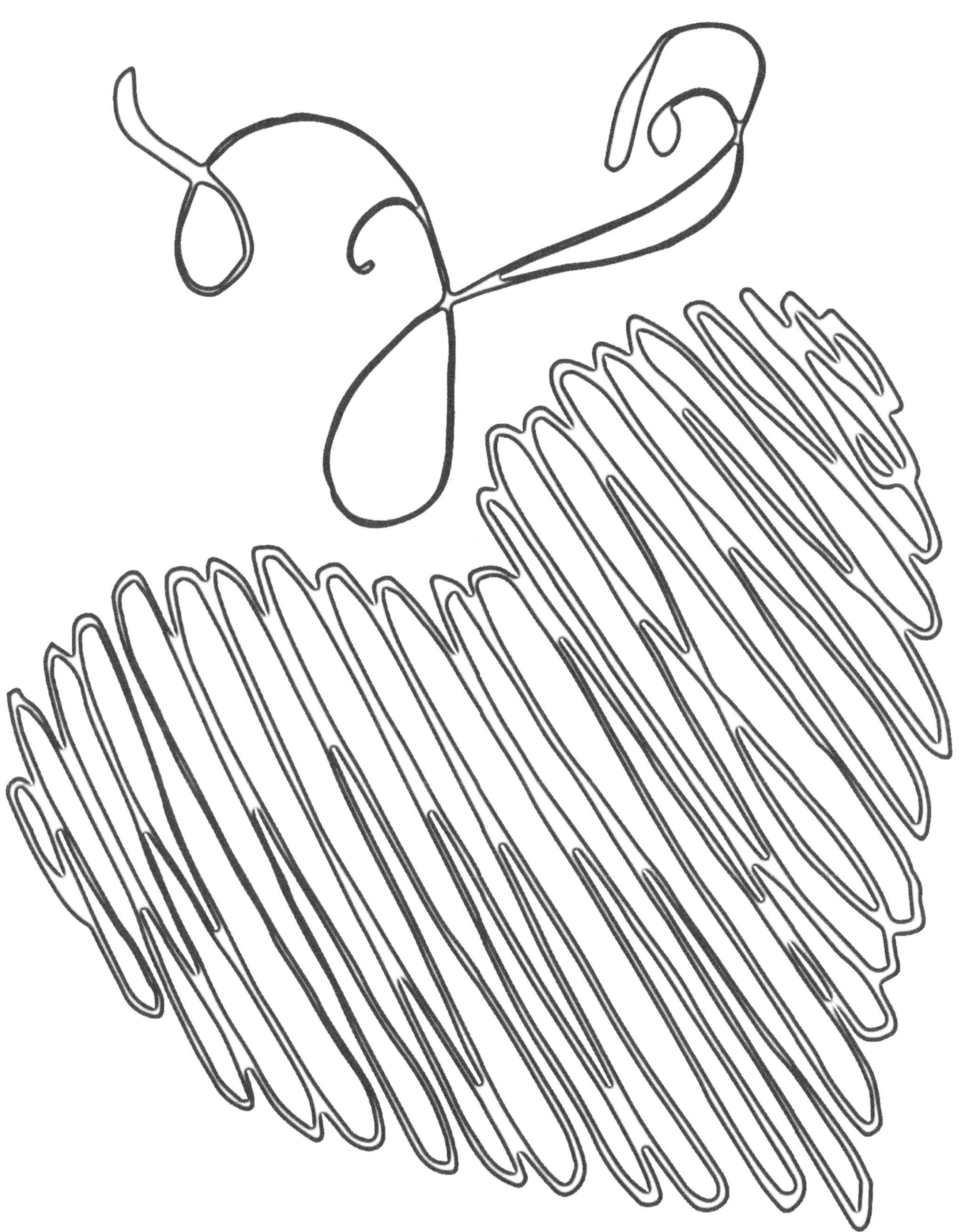

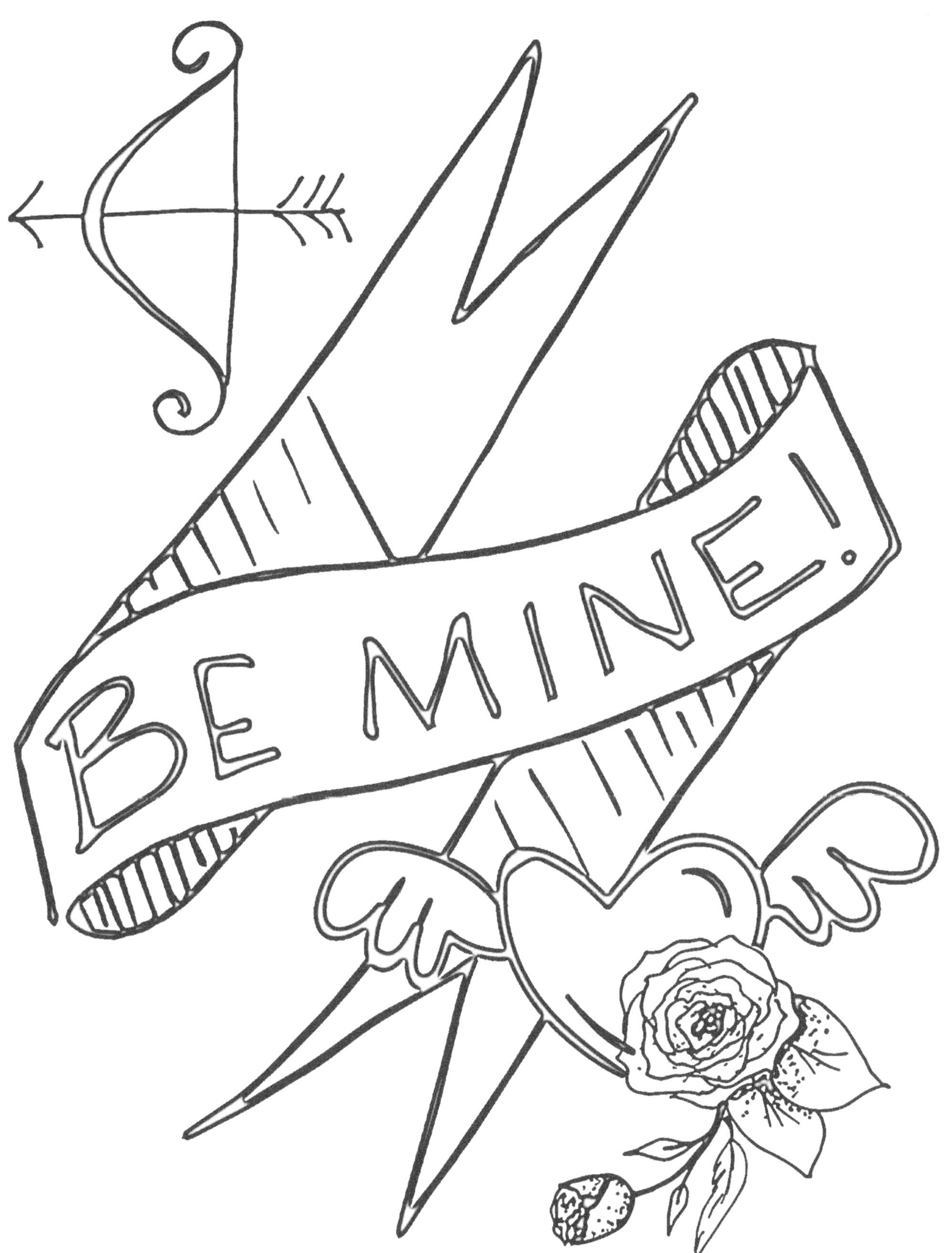
BE MINE!

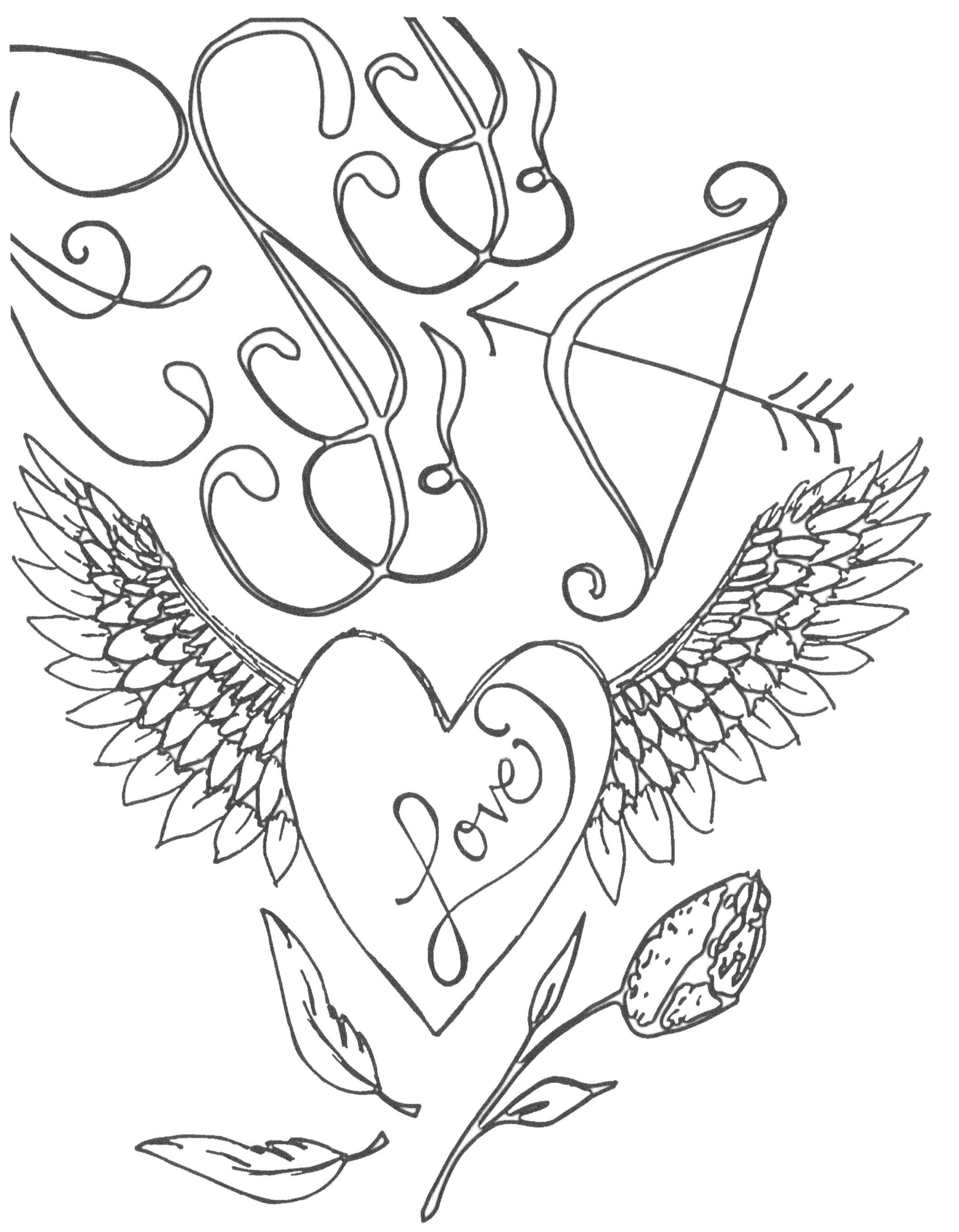
love

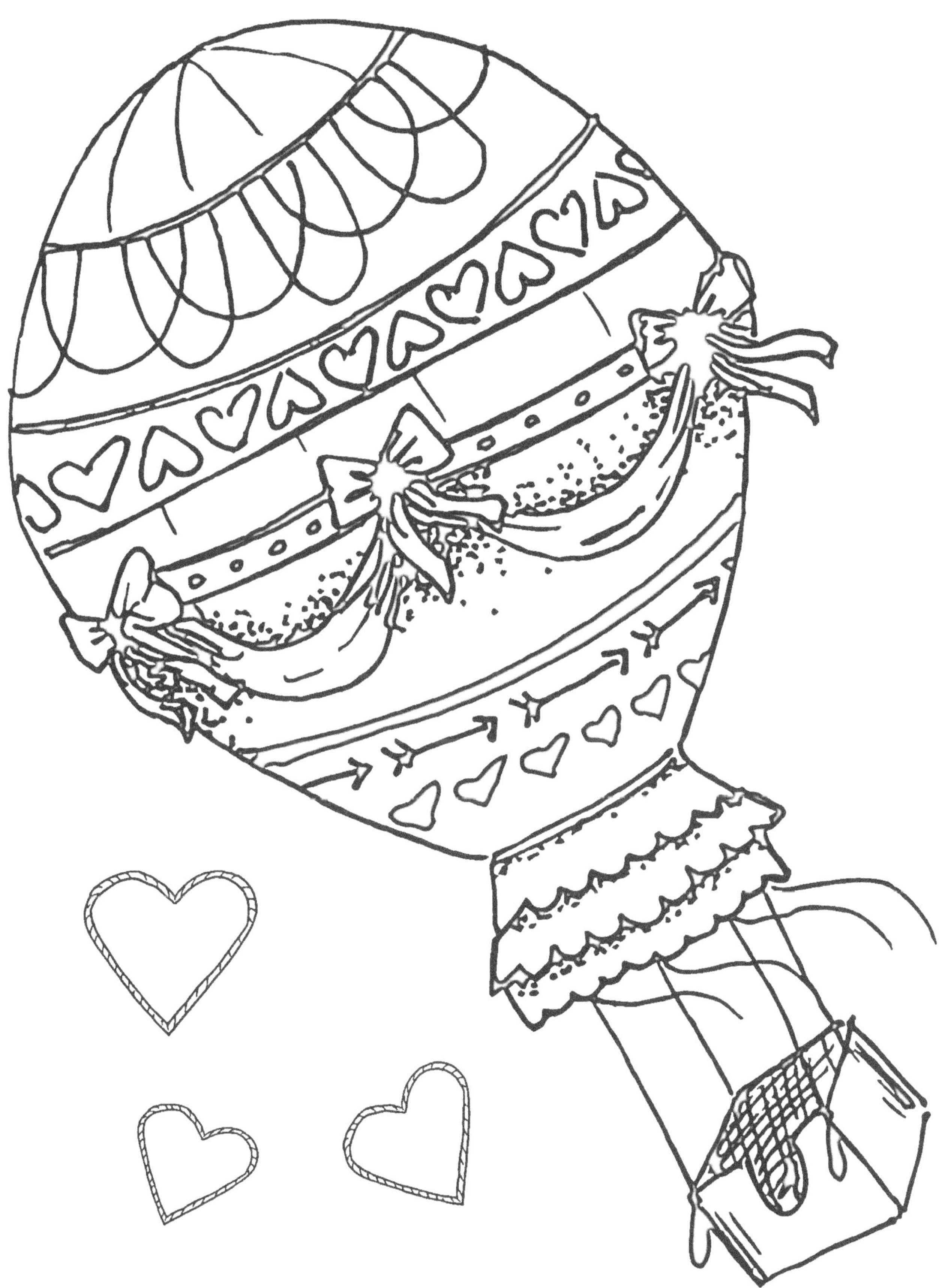

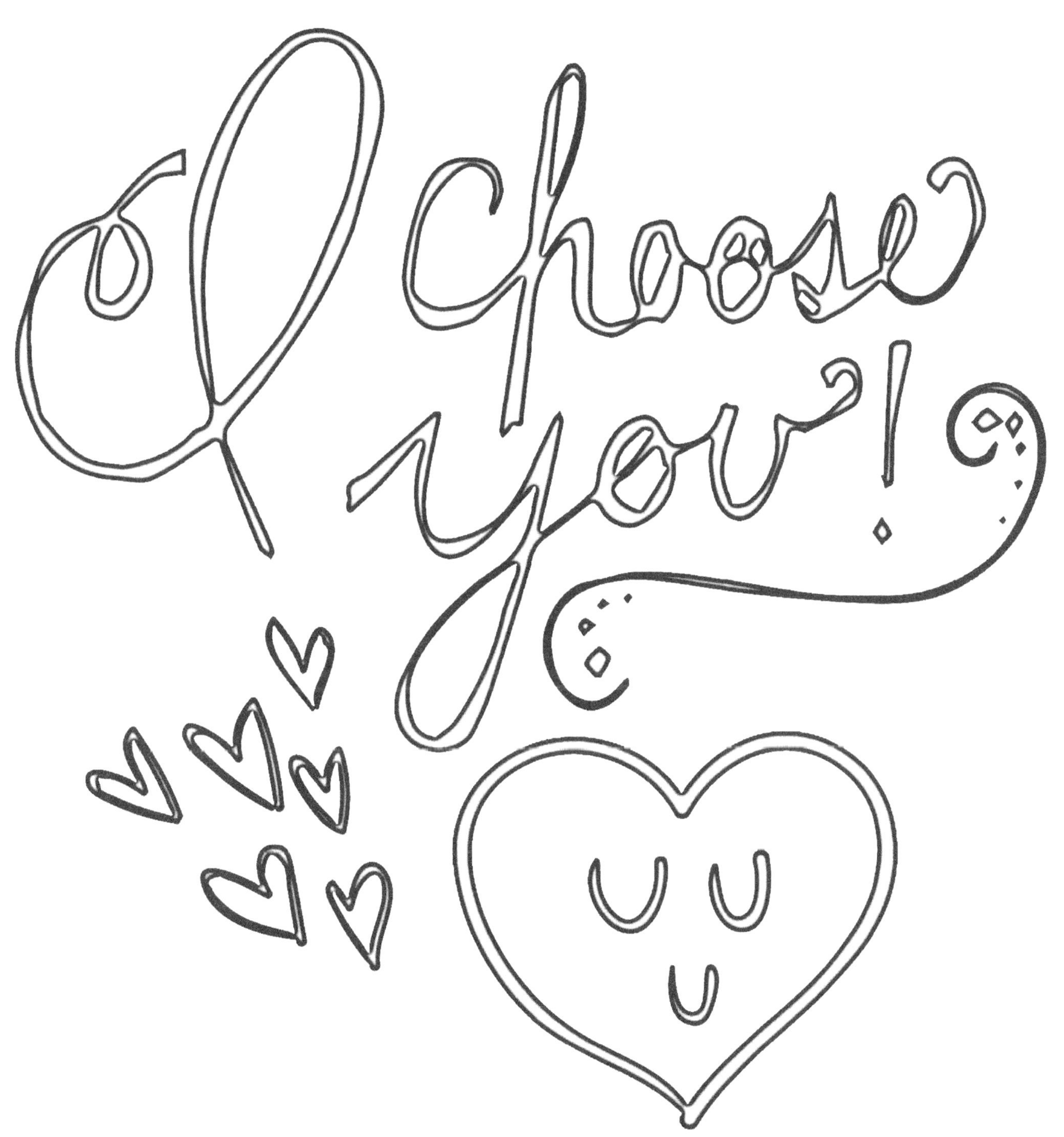

I Choose You!

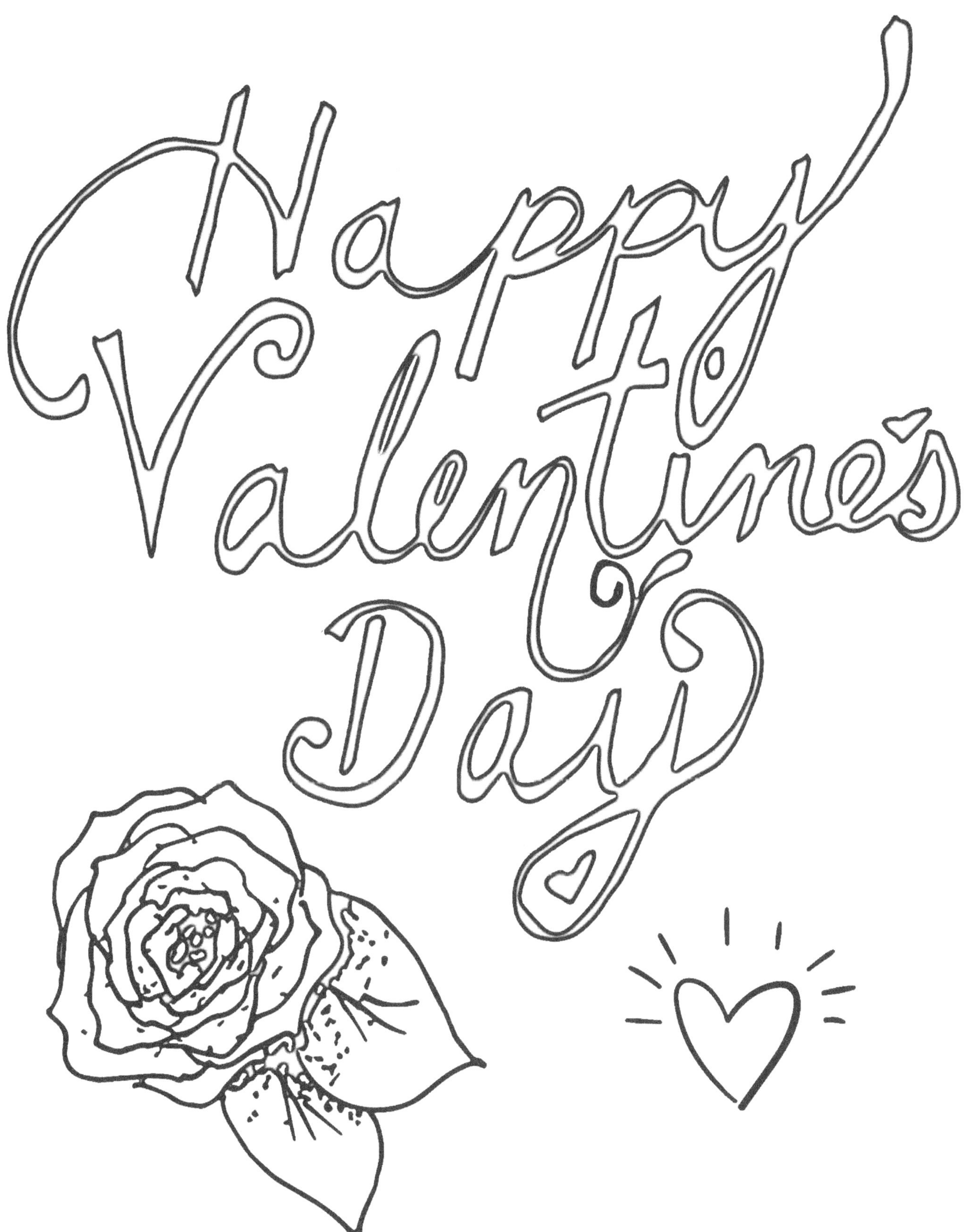

Happy Valentine's Day

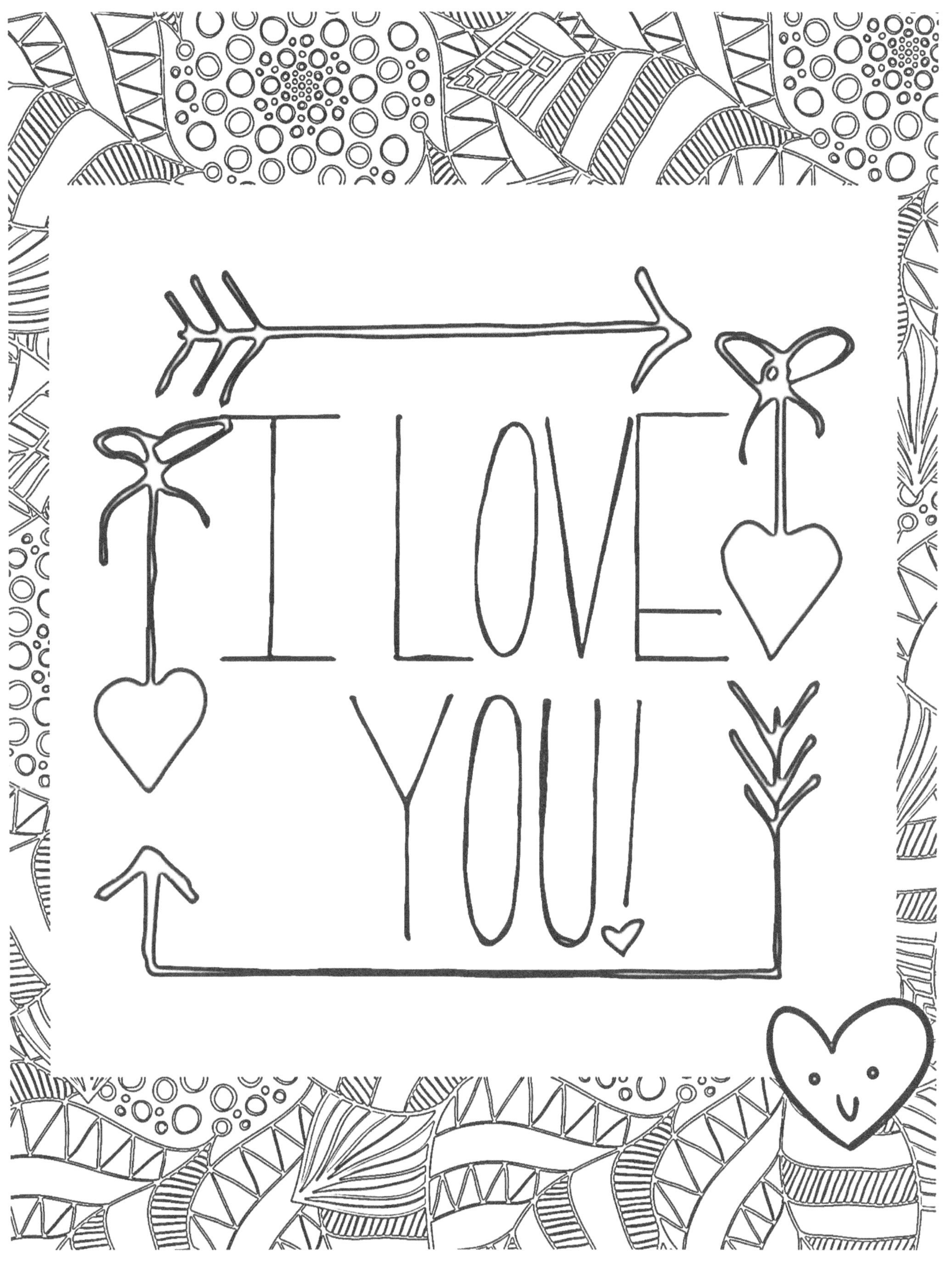

I LOVE YOU!

OVE
14 FEB
LOVE
LOVE
LOVE
14 FEB
XO
XO
XOXO
14

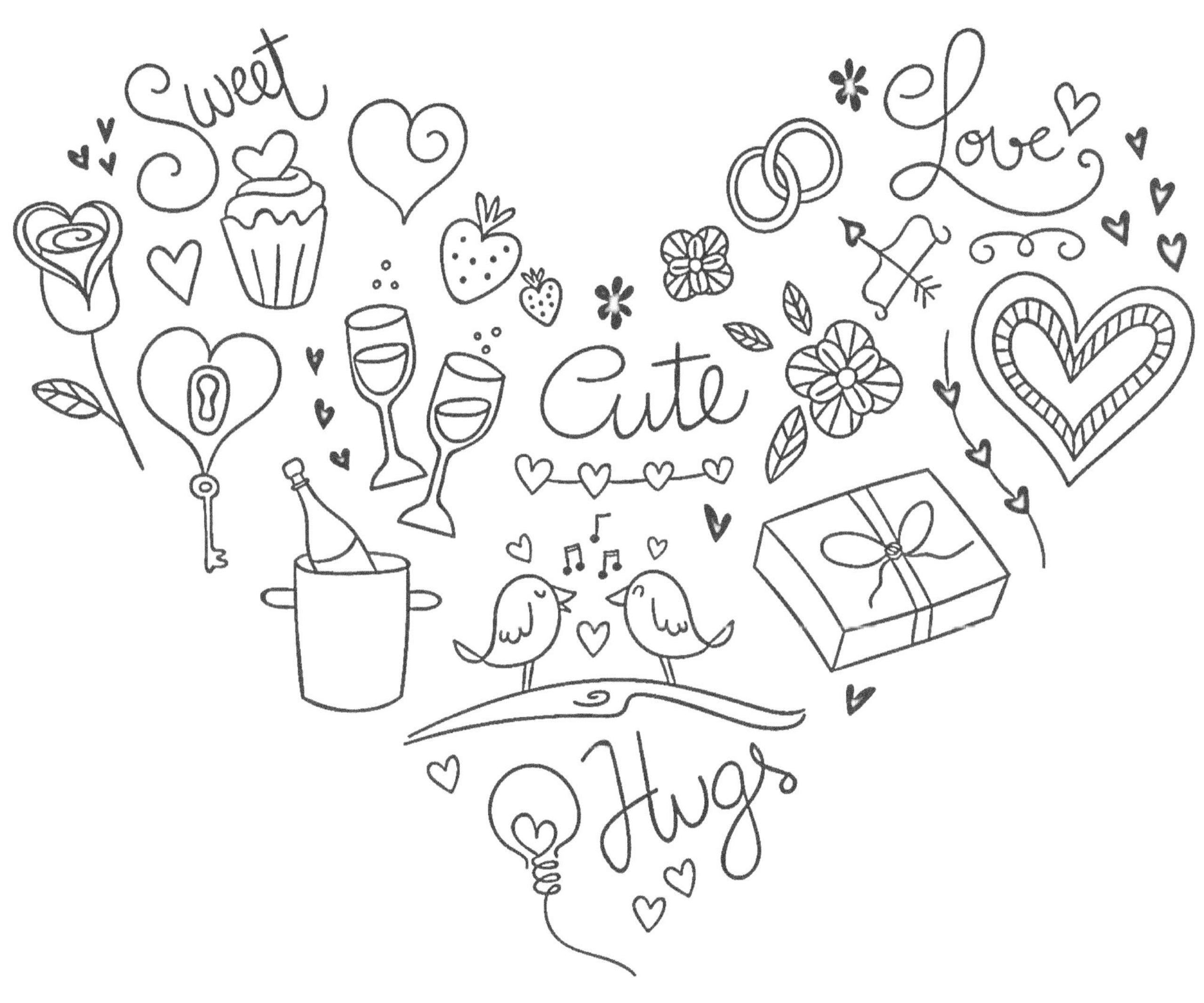

Sweet
Love
Cute
Hugs

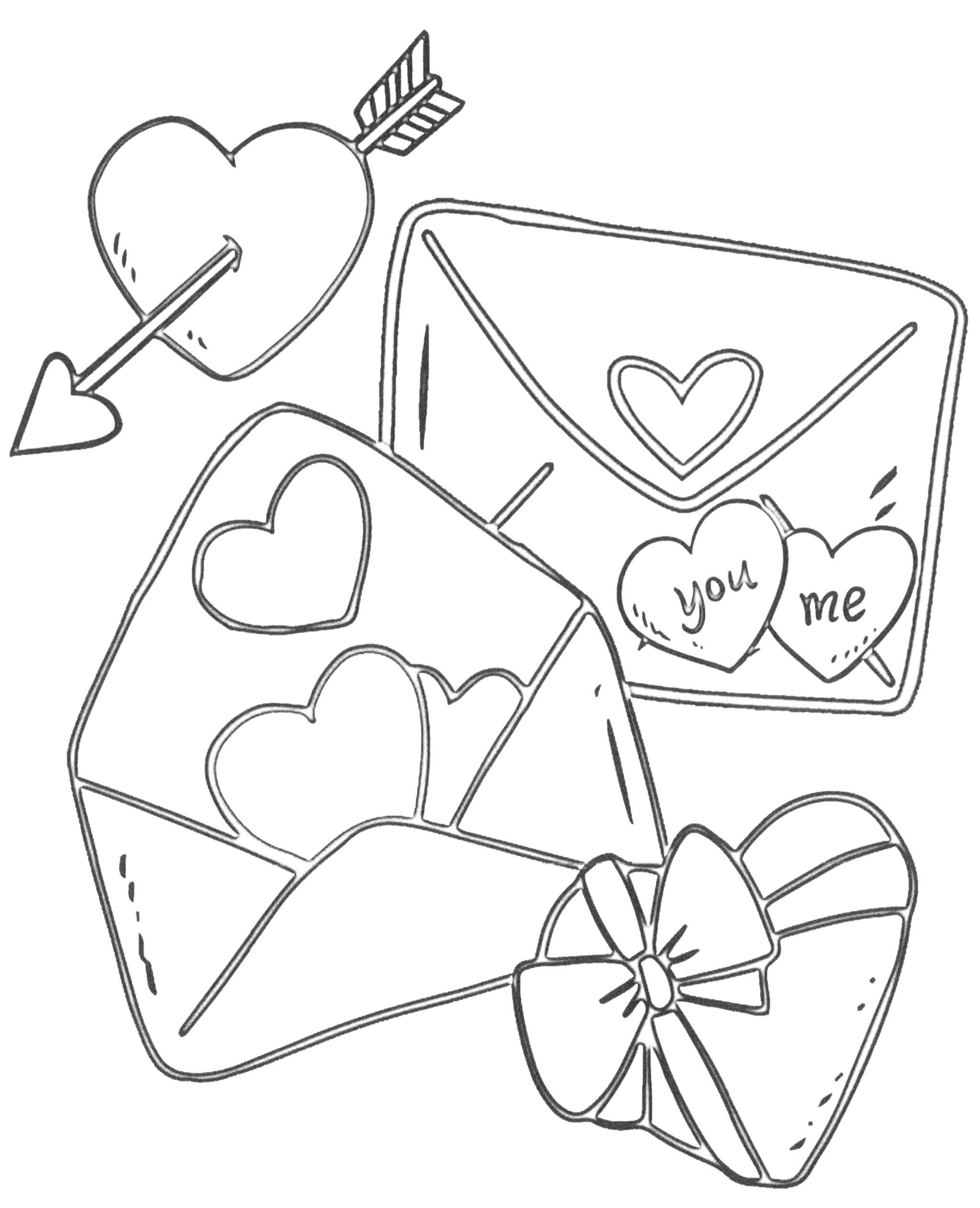

you
me

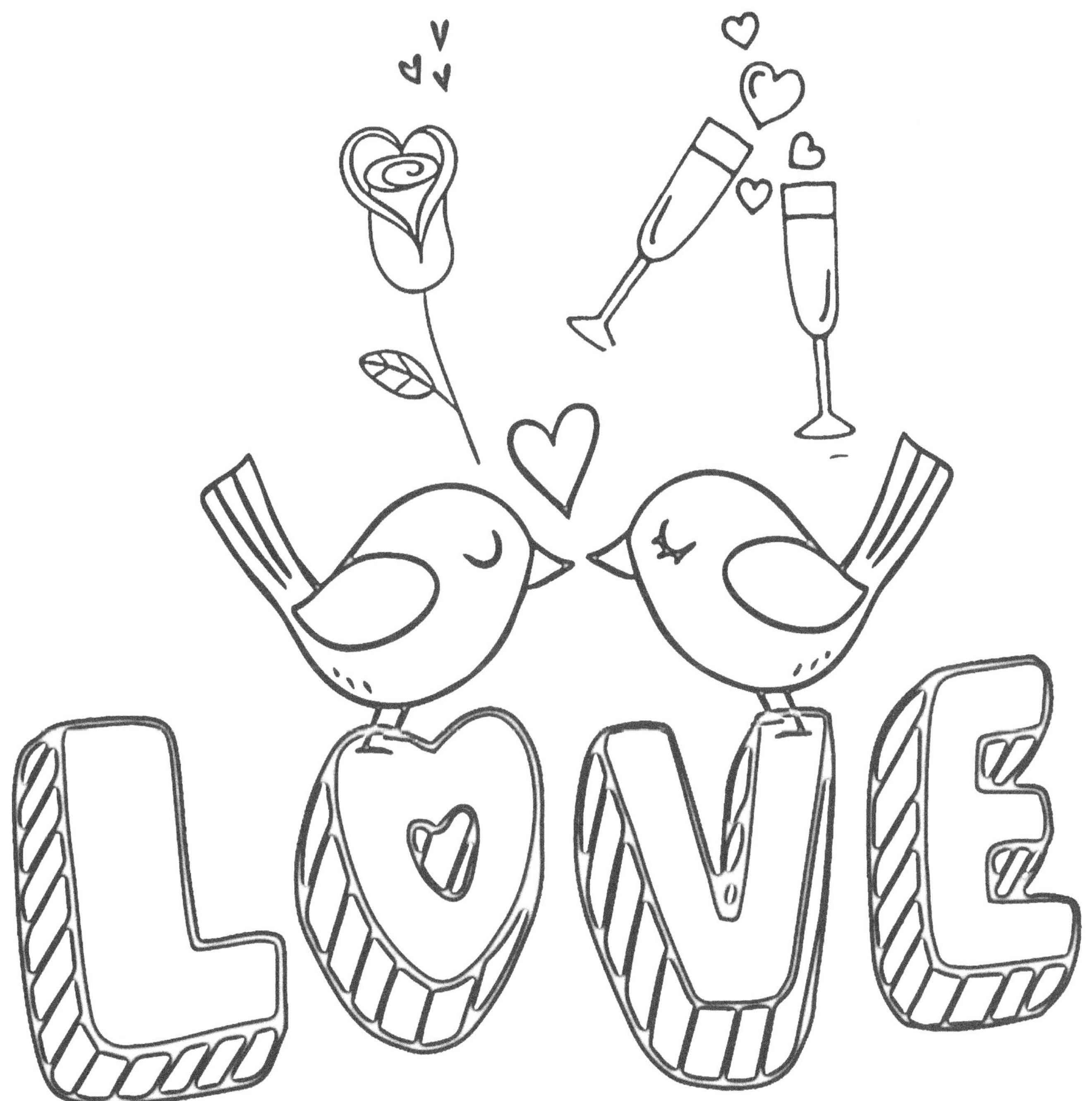

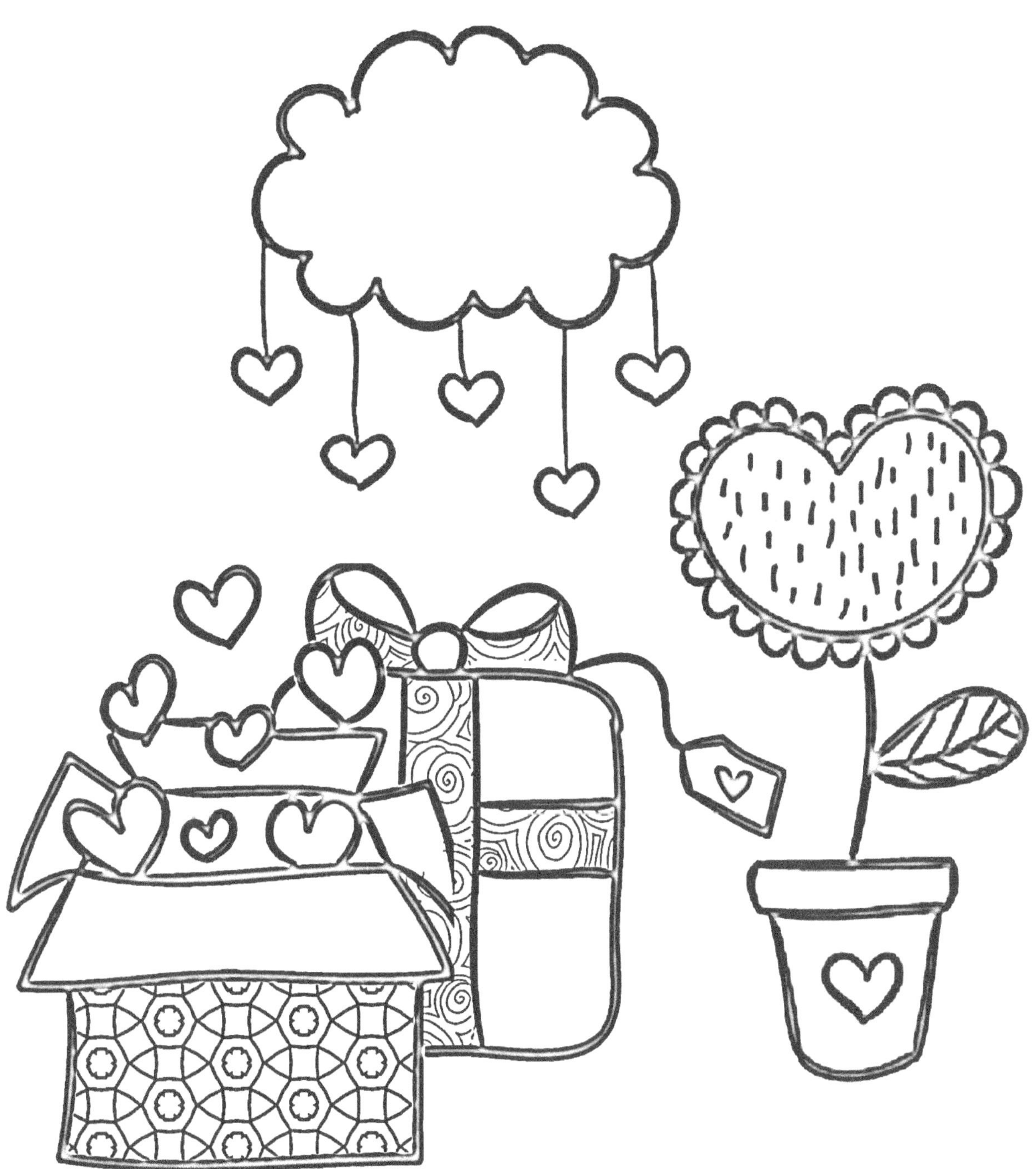

More Books By COLORED DREAMS
(All are available on Amazon)

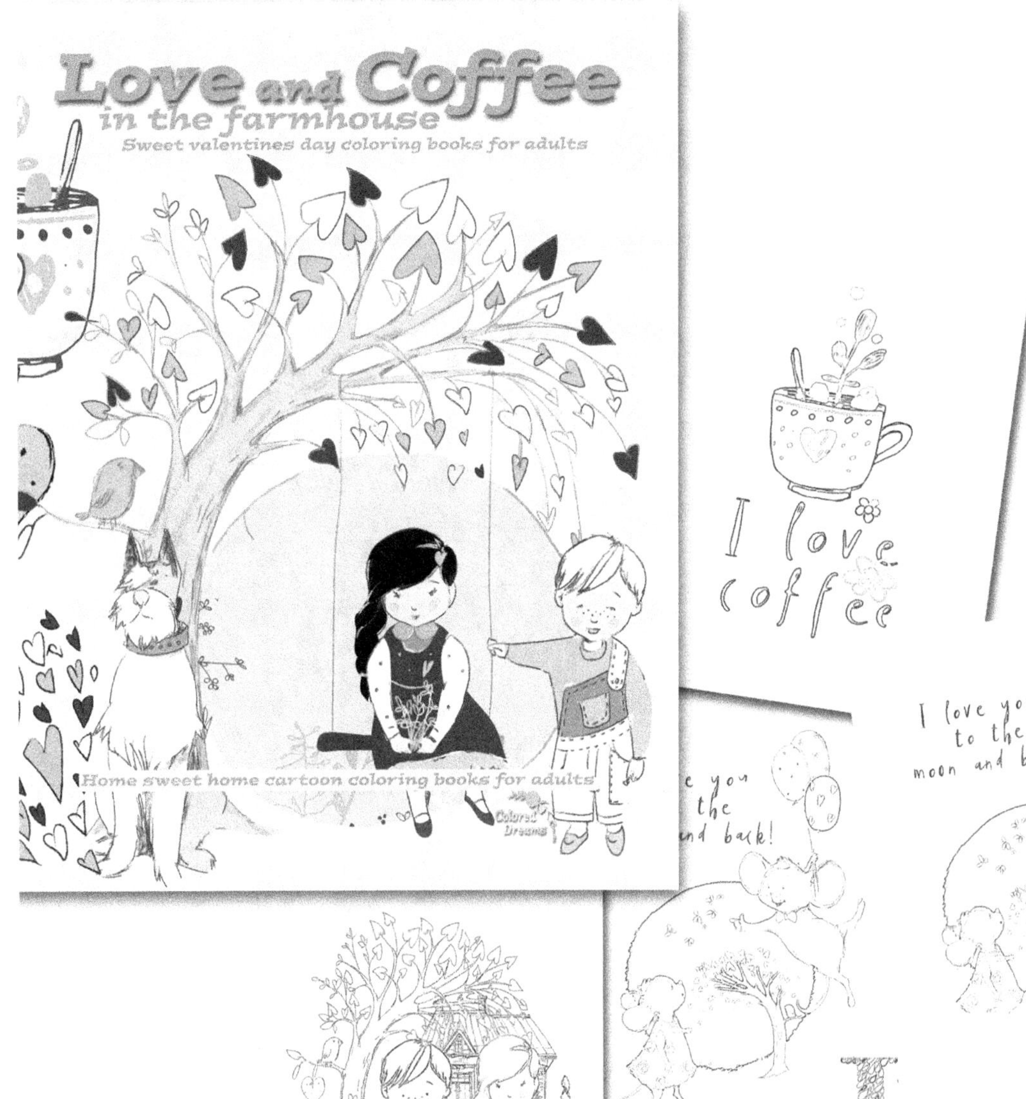

Love and Coffee
in the farmhouse
Sweet valentines day coloring books for adults
Home sweet home cartoon coloring books for adults
Colored Dreams
I love coffee
I love you to the moon and back!
I love you to the moon and back!
I
U

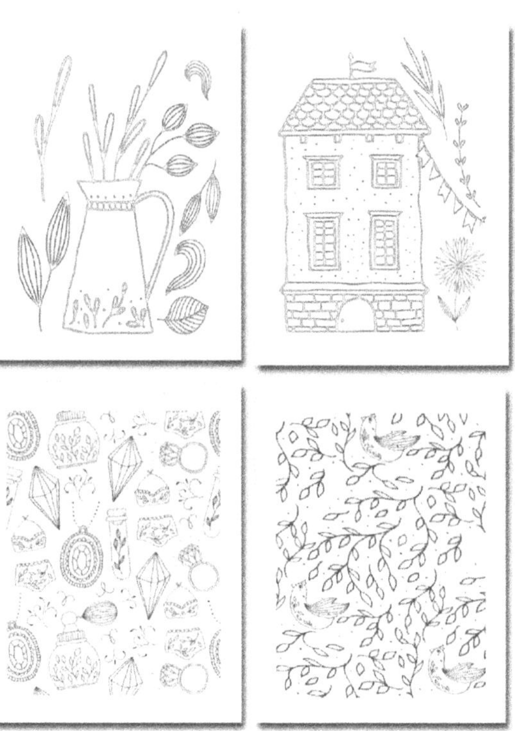

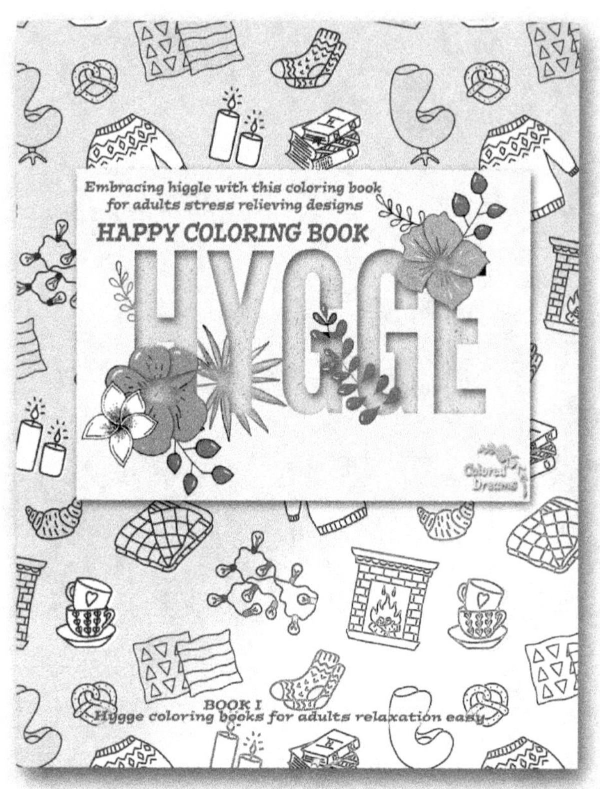
Embracing higgle with this coloring book
for adults stress relieving designs
HAPPY COLORING BOOK
HYGGE
Colored Dreams
BOOK I
Hygge coloring books for adults relaxation easy

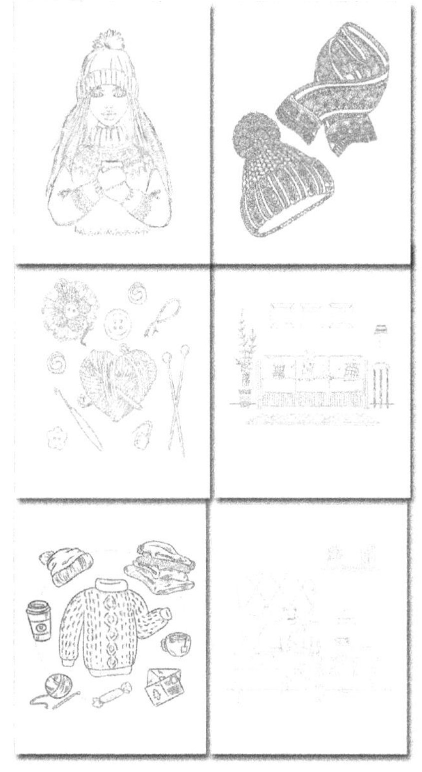

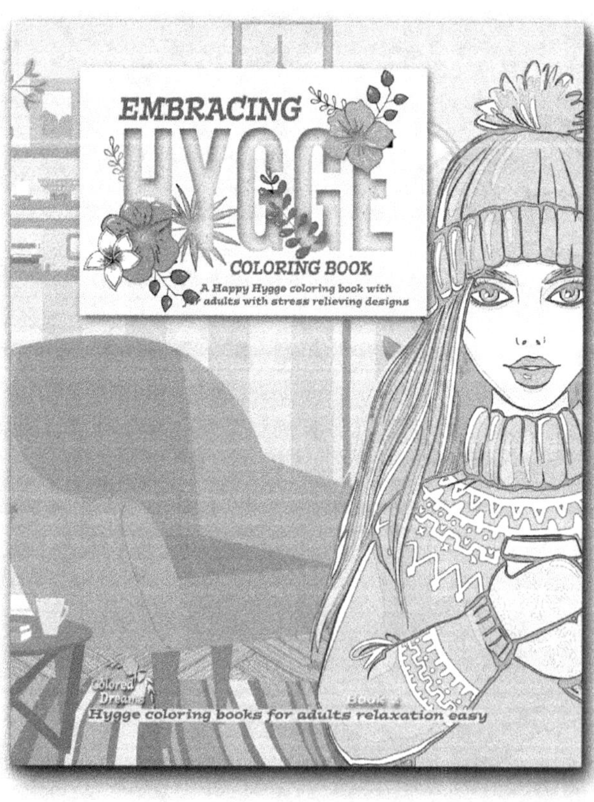
EMBRACING
HYGGE
COLORING BOOK
A Happy Hygge coloring book with
for adults with stress relieving designs
Colored Dreams
Hygge coloring books for adults relaxation easy

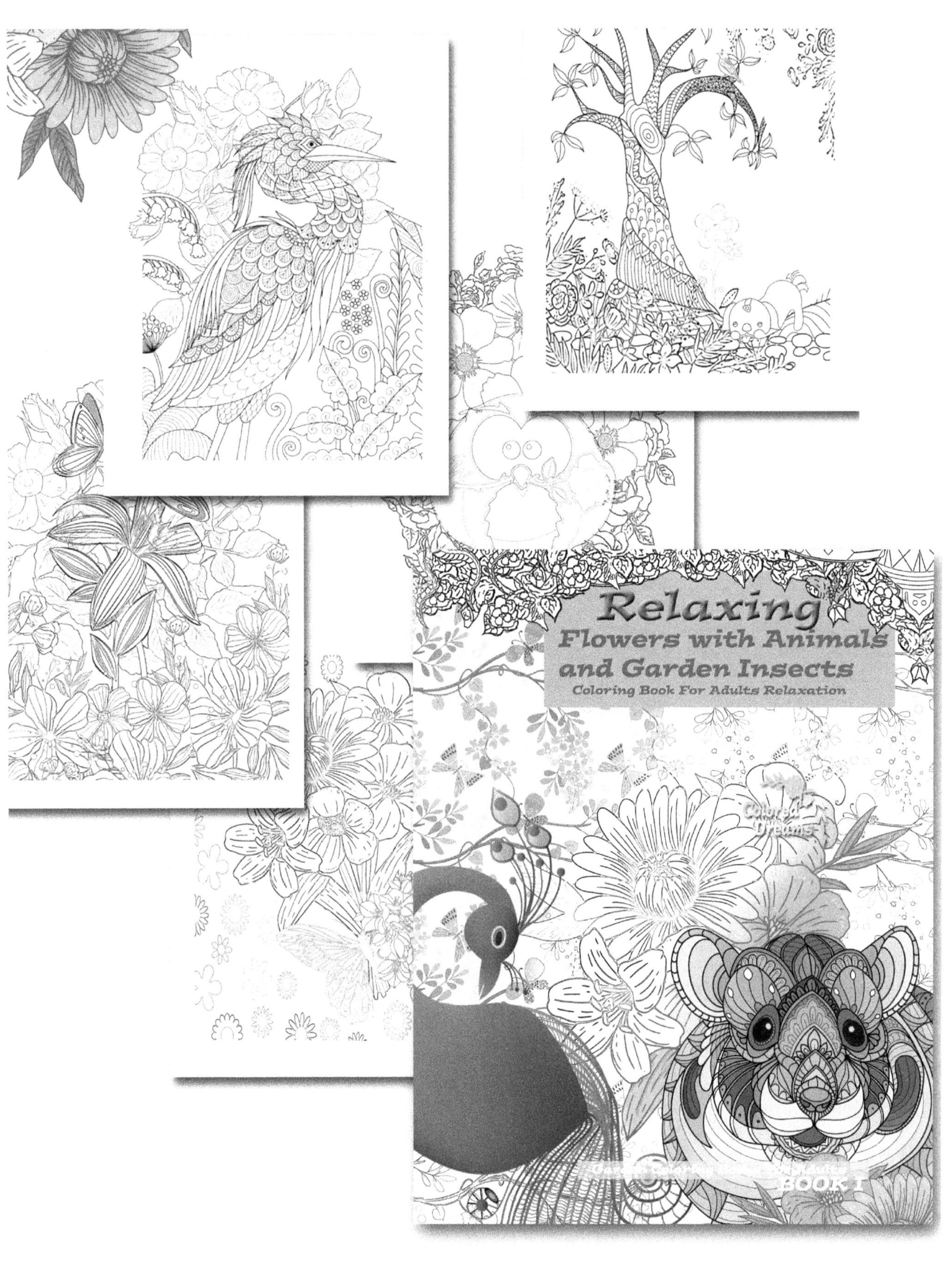

Relaxing
Flowers with Animals
and Garden Insects
Coloring Book For Adults Relaxation
Colored Dreams
BOOK I

Tag your colored pictures with
#vibrantbooks for a change to
get your pictures featured on
our social media

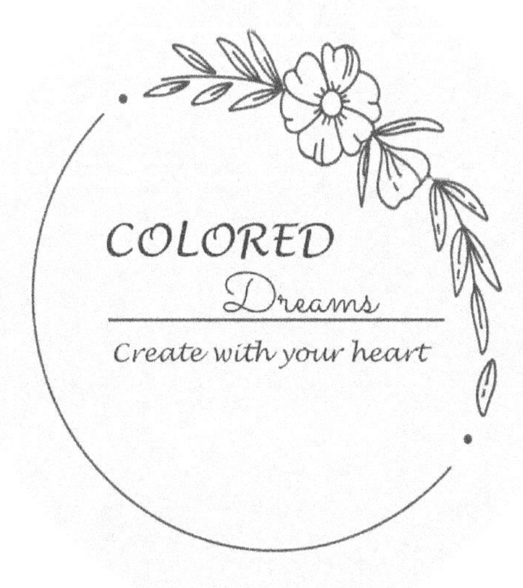

9 784710 768269